AT THE COFFEE TABLE : POEMS

Poems for heal the feelings

Deenabandhu S Adi

First Published in July 2021

ISBN: 978-93-5472-125-0

BLUEROSE PUBLISHERS

www.bluerosepublishers.com

info@bluerosepublishers.com

+91 8882 898 898

Distributed by: BlueRose, Amazon, Flipkart, Shopclues

Love needs your hug...

Hey..., dear my love needs your
sweet hug.
Second innings is started now
with you dear.
May be our love made in heaven.
I remind you everyday in my dream
my dear.
Our love is never ending chapter.
There is feel and romantic sessions have in our love.
Come with me I will take you
another world.
I'm the owner of your all sorrows.
You're the queen of my life ever
my dear.
There will be happen in sweet sessions between me and you.
Hugs are most welcome in love.
Hey dear will you give me your sweet hug everyday...
Come n hug me like my mom.
How our love end without small hug?
Need your beautiful sessions with you....

I'm singing ...

God has composed my

life tune...

Now I'm preparing how to singing...

It's my passion and want to be sing...

Searching for good tune of my life....

There are many tunes but one is match to my life...

Could you guess..?

Yes, that is melody tune..

People always want hear melody songs...

So then I choose my tune...

That is melody tune....

I will give my best in my to everyone...

Because I'm confident in my life....

I have lot of responsibilities on shoulder....

So I will be able give my best...

Hope everyone will take positively....

Want to be good singer of my life...

Dream...

Dreams doesn't to sleep one
who want to achieve.
That getting to him in big position.
Less talk towards now we speak
with our achievement.
Success decides our position
as always. But we must have
kind of kindness that is main
thing to us. Just sit back and
relax some time. You're only
take it Your dreams in the way
of dear friend struggle. Make your dreams colourful.
But don't be sad in anytime. Success always lies in simplicity.
Be humble with every one.
People notice your success
how you react their feelings.
Then your success start to speaking.
Hey get up do make noise with your success.
Don't be sit a silence.
Keep smiling ....

The leader ....

Hey! my leader come up with us.
You're really protect us. Please don't break the chain.
Leader must have positive attitude. Hey leader we're
faith on you but we don't till sun n
moon ends.. We are believe you my
dear leader keep smiling. Victory or
loss is don't take into in your mind.
Have fun with some good works.
Hey leader your 're always be young.
Age is just number don't bother that.
We are waiting for you. Dear leader
I love you. Come on leader....

Depression.......

I felt it very often just
someone insult me. Please
be stay away me because
I already killed by you. Don't
come again in my life. Why you
killed me please tell me ? Did you
know my pains? You are very
dangerous to everyone. Don't be
killed to anyone because they
want to lead a happy life.
Some times you're good,
but basically your presence
is very pained. Why you come
into my life. ..?

My reflection came to visit me....

My reflection came to visit me
and told me first love your self
then you love others.If there is chance
to visit in us that's most luckiest
time to you dear friends. Just know about self and who you are..?and
what's position in society you have.
Simplify your life but don't take
simple way...mirror say You're
beautiful one dear about your
reflection that's most beautiful
answer to you get at the end.
Did you think dear friend once
what are your beautiful works for society?
Just stand in front
of mirror ask to your self.....
Don't bother about your past
your future is most fabulous.
And more bright. Just go,go,go,and go.....
take what you want in your life ?
Enjoy the whole life...without greed's.....
This life is yours and planed by god.
Don't worry about anyone, anything. Always beware In
your behind. Don't trust any one in easily........

Moon.....

Hey moon I need your help
my girl wants to my hug.
Will you say to air flutter as
cool she need a my sweet hug.
That cold air will strong our
relationship.
Between we both have more
strong bound in us. Keep it
strong in long time. Hey moon
her smile is like you because
I gave light to her smile....
Before end of this poem I
confess to her sorry for
everything dear. But my heart
wait's for you always...
Lab.. dab..lab... dab...love you
dear always....

You're my soul....

Hey honey where are you...?
Need your company every time....
Searching you everywhere.
I find you in sea shore,
you're looks like golden girl....
Yes your hairs attractive,
your eyes are dishy...
My baby... Be a my love forever....
My soul....

In your love...

I'm coffee. Just drink me
sip by sip... Your aroma
of love is spreading in me
Hey! Dear your love is more
strong as much...

Death

Unsung life of us deaths
are gives patho songs..
We are loosing our beloved
people, death spread a
palest flowers fragrance...
Beyond the money love is
important to us.

She is happy now...

She is creating happiness
but she hide a untold stories...
She may lost her feelings
for us but she will be strong...
Her feelings are always special
sometimes she sacrifices.

I was fool for you..

Ah...! I was fool for you sometimes cause I love you...

Your love is always best to me my dear Mrs ....

But the real love always lies in tender two hearts...

Dear don't fool me every time because you're my life...

Love stands on only a pure trust my love...

Be heroine in my life dear ...

Don't be like villain my dear...

I pray in god our love be best in world...

He grant to our love be best in world...

The truth

What is truth if i tell death is

mortal to humans. But where we gone

after the death

I want to tell the truth. ##

God was already planned our live

We don't escape anywhere. What we are doing now that's only

counts in heaven how can i tell the truth.##

Truth is immortal of humans life.

If you robb something you couldn't stay as normally. I can say god is stay or your soul can only punish you. This is life truth. ##

God's are never come with us all time.sometimes our inner soul is trying say you are doing wrong thing,need to help every one. But our born was doesn't know the world but we want to achieve something. Then this world will recognize us this is ultimate and universal truth.##

Its about life truth. Read this poem once in your free time. And criticised this. Hope I written best this poem.

Gender bias...

In four walls have want to sex...

But in other time she isn't care...

Why ...? She is also know about everything.

But genders are different some gents have feel good about womens feelings.

Then also men will raped her n her feelings. How they think very brutal... No other ways to rise voice about womens. As in same way whole nation wants to women's empowerment... Where we living in this era...? How we educated..? Yes we have solutions about gender politics... Or gender bias it's equality... Women's also have to free from slavery from men...

We get birth from them but we treat them slave... Why it happen to every ladies...?

They aren't slaves for us...We should also think about them...

Feminism or gender politics never have to see a next generation... We should stop a slave system of on women's...

Yes feminism create a many problems... So we should want a equal society or equality in men & women's....

Your love is like honey...

Your love is like honey
how could i explain without
fragrance of flowers.
Like your love is honey I'm bee
for your fragrance...
Your lips are gives me
naughtiness ideas...
Hey honey be a mine always.

FEELINGS...

THERE IS NO LIMITS FOR THESE

FEELINGS...

EVERY TIME WE ARE FEEL ABOUT LIFE,

FUTURE...

YES ! FEELINGS NEVER COMPROMISE

WITH HUMAN...

OCEAN OF FEELINGS WE HAVE BUT

HOW CAN MANAGE EVERY FEELINGS...?

DON'T HAVE MUCH EXPECTATIONS

EVERYTHING IS UNCERTAIN...

FEELINGS ALSO...

Dreams..

Can't sleeping now.
Because I starve my
hungry dreams...
Thirsty dreams are
always awaken us....
Don't forget your goals
and dreams.
Never ever give up...

The life is like mirror...

Life is like mirror of us
when you stand in
front of mirror
if you laugh it will show
like you. But mirror don't cry...

Mirror always reflection
of us. So the life is also same
what we give to our life that
will returned us...

The life is like mirror...

Life is like mirror of us
when you stand in
front of mirror
if you laugh it will show
like you. But mirror don't cry...

Mirror always reflection
of us. So the life is also same
what we give to our life that
will returned us...

When I see the sun...

When I see the sun i feel
I have energy...

When I see the sun he taught
me wake up and shine like me...

When I see the sun he is symbol
of happiness in loneliness...

He is only a teach be shine
when you're in alone...

Life is short and the way is
long don't take stress...

Just be like sun in every time...

Heal my body...

There no another choice
my sweet lady...
Heal me once cause my love
is always for you...
With sweet hug can make me
pleased me my lady....
Your silence was killed me
talk with me like baby...
Heal my body by your
sweet bee kisses...
love you my lady.....

You never returned...

Uff o, yeah
Don't look back ...
Some where my dead is
calling me...
" Yeah god is calling..."
But at the same time
My body is asking to me ; isn't
we look back...
I said no ..." The whole world
was hurt us" then why we
respond to them...
So I never returned to this
bullshit world.... Bye...bye....
good bye...

Give your solutions...

She is asking now your
solutions why you all hurt
to her...
Just gives your solutions
to her she never lives without
your love...
Can you take her problems....
"No.." Yes we said no... Why
we boys don't give pure
love to her...
Her eyes are full of tears...
"No" ; we should give a
love to her...

Love doesn't have...

Ego with your anger
love her from your
heart not by physic...
Lovers exceptions always
romantic... But it ends with
tragic...
Love your love without anger
and ego...
She will gives you happiness...
Every time she wants to
kiss you...
Every time she wants to
pampering you ...
Don't hurt her / him...

Trees...

Without mother womb how
can we get born...?
Yeah..! Without oxygen how
can we live...?
Trees can only save our
life doctors are mange our
healthy status, but the end
tress are valuable asset for
society...
Don't cut the trees...
How can you live without air
dear human.. Stop tree
sectorial keep protect our
valuable asset...

Dance because...

Dance extract your feelings
and Talent.
Hey dear talent don't prove
your talent to others make a
way on your success path...
Just dance once in day it's heal
to all your anger, sad moods...
Just on your tv , start your
dance...

Shine with success...

Be a achiever with some
humanity...
Without humanity you're
nothing dude...
When you speak without struggle
there is no chance to shine.
Just make way of your way
like sun..
Have a beautiful journey
ahead for you... Achiever...

Some secretes are take you
on higher position... Sh!

Beautiful nature...

Ah...! Such sounds have nature
but we shouldn't know the respect
of nature.
But always nature looks beautiful.
Nature never spoil our life.
Hey human don't spoil nature.
Beyond the nature we aren't
doesn't anything...
Then why you cut the trees...
Before you think trees are your future...

She won't hurt to you.

May be her replies are late
but she won't hurt you.
Hey men try to understand
her feelings, don't be too rude.
Every time she was lose,
but once wouldn't win...
Be a kind with her, she won't
lose you...an never try to hurt you....

Life is theater...

We enact by god rules.
But we knows about our limits.
Hey god you're planed our life
but you ain't restricted us...
But Put a limits to us..
Because of we are actors...
In this life theatre.

My love....

She is like baby for me...

Yes ! She is world for me ...

Her innocence like pure water...

How can I elaborate your beauty

dear... Just you're incomparable to

anything my dear....

Love you till my last breath...

You will live in me forever.....

Stars are symbols of..

You were everywhere...
Stars are symbolic of our life...
How we put more efforts in
our life we will be shine more...
Those are shine by moon like
our life shines by our efforts ...

So, be a worth to everyone...

Room no - 120 (Horror poem)

That room was preceded
with full of blood. ... (
She was screaming n laughing...
But no one have to dare
open the door...
Yeaa she hang with herself...
When she was young she
was happy... Hey guys don't
disrespect her feelings...
Yes she is victim of rape....
Still no one open that room.....
Because that is have more
curious things....

Beyond the darkness

Hide a secret light ....
Just we search for that...
Without struggling or dark,light or
success never get.
That's why beyond the darkness
light is there for us...
Be hope in every second, that is life
plus point...

Smile in every time...

Don't hide your smile...

It's weapon to your enemy.

Behave like fool but think

like matured.

In your smile have type of attitude...

Your smile can change

someone's mood.

Be a rich in your think ...

Have great gratitude in

your smile...

Be a favorite to all....

Noise of screaming...

Someone calling me
in midnight...
Oh yes she is dead ! But her
noise screaming voice is
having painful.
Yes she is victim of rape...
She talk to me every
midnight...:(Her crying eyes
feel with a pain ...Yes will get
her own justice one day....
I will there for you ...
My dear friend...

Dreams are like stars...

Shine by moon
but dreams are alive
every time.
Dreamed big not
just small.
Your ways make you be
a proud....

My honey's kiss....

Hey my lady the day is set
Just hug me for love.
Show me the love of yours.
The bee will around you
cause you're my honey.
Just love me all time
my honey is never fails
in her love ....That why
she cares me n kiss me like
mom.... Love you honey...

Black heart...

There is black poison in
my heart when you're cheated
me it'll burst out.
Hey baby don't cheat me
I am already hurtful.
Black is great colour for
great persons.
So be a loved by me.
I love you ever....

Walking alone...

Just go...go... Long way a go..
May be the world will end but
peace is never meet you...
Alone walks make me emotional.
But the teach me a lot...
To be alone with happy
of your self-respect...
Just walk in night alone on
empty roads. Miles are speaks
with you...

www.ingramcontent.com/pod-product-compliance
Ingram Content Group UK Ltd.
Pitfield, Milton Keynes, MK11 3LW, UK
UKHW040014200726
13854UKWH00001B/188

9 789354 721250